Crafts For Kids

To Give As Gifts

Copyright © 2024 by Little Creations Press. Illustrated by Haley Matthews

All rights reserved. Power Of Yet LLC

First Printing, 2024 ISBN 978-3-948298-26-5

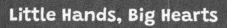

Little Hands, Big Hearts

Welcome to a **world** where imagination meets creation, a place where little hands make big impressions. This book is a treasure trove of simple, yet beautiful crafts designed for toddlers to create and for loved ones to cherish. Each page is an invitation to explore creativity and to strengthen the bonds of love through the joy of crafting.

As parents, we often search for ways to bridge the gap between the eagerness of our little ones to create and our desire to have keepsakes that are meaningful and display-worthy. This collection of crafts is the answer. From the colorful pasta necklace to the Modern Rock Cactus Pot, every project is tailored for young children, ensuring that the process is as enjoyable as the end result.

These crafts are more than just activities; they are opportunities for learning, for laughter, and for creating memories. They are a way for children to express their love and creativity, resulting in gifts that are as unique as the little hands that made them. This book is for every parent who cherishes the magic of their child's imagination and for every grandparent, teacher, and loved one who appreciates a heartfelt, handmade gift.

As you turn each page, you and your child will embark on a journey of creativity. Each craft is a story waiting to be told, a special moment waiting to be shared. So, gather your materials, hold those little hands, and let's start this beautiful journey of making crafts that come straight from the heart.

Modern Rock Cactus Pot

Materials

* Smooth river rocks or pebbles
* Green acrylic paint
* White paint for details
* Small flower pot
* Sand or small pebbles for pot filling

Instructions

1. Paint the rocks green and let them dry.

2. Use white paint to add details resembling cactus spikes.

3. Fill the flower pot with sand or small pebbles.

4. Once the painted rocks are dry, arrange them on top of the sand in the pot.

5. **Optional:** Add a small flower embellishment on one of the rocks.

This creates a cute, low-maintenance "cactus" that can sit on a desk or shelf.

Black Ring Canvas Art

Materials

* White canvas
* One color of non-toxic acrylic paint for the background
* Black non-toxic acrylic paint for the rings
* A small drinking glass or cup
* Paint brushes or sponge brushes
* Newspapers or a drop cloth
* Paper plates or a paint palette

Instructions

1. **Setup:** Cover the work area with newspapers or a drop cloth to protect surfaces. Dress the toddler in old clothes or a smock.

2. **Paint the Background:** Using a paintbrush or sponge brush, help the toddler to paint the entire canvas in one solid, vibrant color. Ensure the color is evenly spread across the surface. Let it dry completely.

3. **Prepare the Rings:** Pour black paint onto a paper plate. Dip the backside of the glass into the black paint, ensuring it's fully coated.

4. **Stamp the Rings:** Guide the toddler to press the painted glass onto the canvas to create rings. Allow them to make 4 uneven rings, reapplying the paint to the glass as needed.

5. **Add Details:** Let the toddler use their fingers or a paintbrush to add additional black paint splashes around the rings for a playful effect.

6. **Dry:** Set the canvas aside to dry completely.

7. **Display:** Once dry, hang the canvas against a plain white background to make the colors pop and give the room a touch of modern art made with love by a toddler.

Bottle Cap Mural

Materials

* A large piece of cardboard or wood panel
* Bottle caps in various colors (can be painted)
* Non-toxic glue
* Hammer and nails (optional, for a more permanent fixture)

Instructions

1. If the bottle caps aren't already colored, paint them and let them dry.

2. Lay out your bottle caps on the board to create a design or pattern.

3. Glue the caps down or use a hammer and nails to affix them for a more 3D effect.

4. Once complete, this mural can be a vibrant piece of art for any room.

Clay Cookie Ornament

Materials

* Air-dry clay
* Non-toxic acrylic paint (various colors)
* Paintbrushes
* Ribbon or string for hanging
* Rolling pin (optional)
* Cookie cutters (optional)

Instructions

1. **Shape the Clay:** Help your toddler take a small amount of air-dry clay and shape it into a round disc, similar to a cookie. It doesn't have to be perfectly round or flat — the unevenness adds character. You can also use a rolling pin to flatten the clay and cookie cutters to shape it, but doing it by hand is more fun for toddlers.

2. **Let it Dry:** Place the clay 'cookies' on a flat surface and let them dry according to the clay's instructions, usually about 24 hours. Make sure they are completely dry before painting.

3. **Paint the Cookie:** Now the fun part! Let your toddler use non-toxic acrylic paints to decorate the clay cookies. They can try to mimic their favorite cookies, like chocolate chip or sugar cookies with icing and sprinkles. Encourage them to be creative.

4. **Add Ribbon or String:** Once the paint is dry, you can make a small hole at the top of the clay cookie (if not done before drying) and thread a ribbon or string through it. This allows the ornament to be hung up as a decoration.

5. **Gift It:** Now your toddler's handmade clay cookie ornament is ready to be gifted to a baking enthusiast. It's a unique and personal gift that any baker would cherish.

This craft is a great way for toddlers to explore their creativity and make something special for someone they care about. Enjoy crafting together!

Colorful Button Canvas

Materials

* A white canvas
* Assorted colorful buttons
* Non-toxic glue

Instructions

1. Sort the buttons by color with your toddler.

2. Apply glue to the canvas in the shape of a simple image or pattern, like a heart or a tree.

3. Have your toddler place the buttons on the glue to fill in the shape.

4. Let it dry to create a textured and colorful piece of art.

Miniature Golf Course in a Box

Materials

* A shallow cardboard box (like a shoebox)
* Green felt or fabric (to represent grass)
* Small objects to use as obstacles (like blocks, small toys, or bottle caps)
* Golf tees or small sticks
* A ping pong ball or a small golf balls
* Non-toxic glue
* Scissors (for adult use)

Instructions

1. **Prepare the Box:** Place the green felt or fabric inside the box, covering the bottom to represent grass. Glue it down so it stays in place.

2. **Create Obstacles:** Help your toddler arrange and glue small objects inside the box to serve as obstacles on the golf course. These can be placed randomly for a fun layout.

3. **Add Tees:** Place a few golf tees or small sticks standing upright in the box. These can act as starting points for each 'hole' of the mini-golf course.

4. **Golf Ball:** Use a ping pong ball or a small lightweight ball as the golf ball.

5. **Play Mini-Golf:** Once the glue has dried, your child can use a small stick or finger to push the ball around the obstacles, mimicking a game of mini-golf.

6. **Gifting:** The Miniature Golf Course in a Box is now ready to be gifted to a golf enthusiast. It's a playful representation of the sport that can also double as a fun, interactive toy.

This craft allows toddlers to work on their fine motor skills and spatial awareness while creating a unique and thoughtful gift.

Fork Abstract Painting

Materials

* White canvas or heavy-weight white paper
* Non-toxic acrylic paints in various colors
* Newspapers or a drop cloth to protect the work surface
* Forks (plastic or metal)
* Palette or paper plates to hold paint
* Smock or old clothes for the child
* Wet wipes or a cloth for clean-up

Instructions

1. **Setup:** Spread newspapers or a drop cloth over the work surface where the child will paint. Place the white canvas or paper on the work area. Squirt small amounts of different colored paints onto a palette or paper plates.

2. **Painting with Forks:** Show the child how to dip the backside of the fork into the paint. Let them experiment with making different lines and textures by pressing and dragging the fork across the canvas.

3. **Creating Textures:** Encourage the child to use the tines of the fork to make lines, swirls, and dot patterns. They can use the side of the fork to scrape across the paint for a different effect.

4. **Adding Splashes:** If the child is enthusiastic, they can flick paint onto the canvas with the fork for a splattered effect. They can also use their fingers to add additional splatters or to mix colors directly on the canvas.

5. **Layering:** Allow the first layer of paint to dry a bit if possible. Then, they can add more layers on top, which will add depth to the painting.

6. **Finishing Touches:** Once the child is satisfied with their painting, set it aside to dry completely.

7. **Display:** When the painting is dry, you can display it as is or put it in a frame without glass to showcase the texture.

Note: This activity can get messy, so make sure to dress the child in old clothes and keep wet wipes or a damp cloth handy for quick clean-up of hands and any spills.

These instructions are designed to give the child plenty of freedom to explore and express themselves through painting, resulting in a unique piece of art that can be proudly displayed at home.

14

Seed Mosaic Art

Materials

* A variety of seeds (sunflower seeds, pumpkin seeds, lentils, beans, etc.)
* Cardboard or a thick piece of paper as a base
* Non-toxic glue
* A small bowl of water (to soften harder seeds, if necessary)
* Wax paper (to work on and to prevent sticking)

Instructions

1. **Preparation:** Begin by sorting the seeds into different bowls by type and size. This can be a fun activity for the child to help with.

2. **Design Planning:** Decide on a design or pattern for your mosaic. This could be anything from a simple shape like a heart or a more complex picture like a flower or animal. Draw a rough outline of the design onto the cardboard with a pencil.

3. **Gluing Process:** Start gluing the seeds onto the cardboard within the outline of your design. For younger children, they might just enjoy placing seeds randomly or in simple patterns. Apply glue to a small area to start with so it doesn't dry out before the seeds are placed.

4. **Creating the Mosaic:** Place the seeds onto the glue one by one. Use the bigger seeds to fill larger areas and the smaller seeds to add detail. You can create texture by layering seeds or using different types to create a pattern. Let the child place the seeds. The design doesn't have to be perfect — the beauty is in the uniqueness of their creation.

5. **Drying:** Once the design is complete, leave the mosaic flat to dry completely.

This Seed Mosaic Art project allows children to explore their creativity while engaging in a sensory activity. Plus, they'll have a beautiful piece of art to show for their efforts!

Whimsical Washi Tape Candle Decor

Materials

✳ Plain glass candles (simple, unscented candles in a glass container)

✳ Washi tape in various colors and patterns

✳ Scissors

Instructions

1. **Select Washi Tapes:** Begin by letting your child pick out their favorite washi tapes. A variety of colors and patterns can make this craft more fun and playful.

2. **Cutting Tape:** Depending on the child's age and skill level, an adult might need to help cut the tape into strips. Strips can vary in length for a more dynamic look.

3. **Decorate the Glass:** Show your child how to wrap the strips of washi tape around the glass part of the candle. Encourage them to overlap the tapes and mix patterns in an imaginative way.

4. **Apply Tape:** If your child is very young, they might place the tape unevenly or create wrinkles — and that's okay! It adds to the whimsical charm of the craft.

5. **Finishing Touches:** Once the glass is covered to their satisfaction, smooth down any particularly loose ends of tape.

6. **Display Your Candle:** Place the newly decorated candle on a table or shelf. It will not only serve as a charming piece of decor but also as a proud display of your child's creativity.

Note: Always supervise children during this craft, especially if using scissors or lighting the candle.

This craft is not about perfection but celebrating the creative and unique ways children see and decorate the world around them.

Nature Collage Canvas

Materials

* A blank canvas
* Non-toxic glue
* Collected nature items (leaves, twigs, pressed flowers)
* Clear sealant (optional)

Instructions

1. Go on a nature walk with your toddler and collect various items.

2. Back at home, arrange the items on the canvas in a pleasing design.

3. Glue the items down and let it dry.

4. Apply a clear sealant to preserve the natural elements.

Painted Flower Pot

Materials

* A plain terracotta flower pot
* Non-toxic acrylic paints in various colors
* Paintbrushes
* Newspaper or a drop cloth

Instructions

1. **Preparation:** Spread out the newspaper or drop cloth to protect your work surface. Place the flower pot on top.

2. **Painting:** Give your child the paintbrushes and paints. Let them freely paint the pot in whatever colors and patterns they choose. Encourage creativity and don't worry about messiness.

3. **Adding Details:** They can use their fingers or the back of the brush to add dots, lines, or other simple decorations.

4. **Drying:** Allow the paint to dry completely. This may take a few hours.

5. **Sealing (Optional):** Once dry, you can seal the paint with a clear acrylic spray to protect it. This step should be done by an adult in a well-ventilated area.

6. **Planting:** Once everything is dry, the pot is ready to be used for a plant.

This activity is a fun way for children to express their creativity and contribute to home decor in their own unique way. The 'ugly' aspect is part of the charm, showcasing the uninhibited and joyful creativity of a child.

Sugar Scrub

Materials

* 1 cup granulated sugar
* 1/4 cup organic coconut oil
* 1/2 teaspoon sugar sprinkles
* 6 drops of vanilla essential oil (or any preferred scent)
* Mixing bowl
* Spoon or spatula for mixing
* Small container for storing the scrub

Instructions

1. **Mix Dry Ingredients:** In the bowl, let the child combine the granulated sugar with the sugar sprinkles.

2. **Add Wet Ingredients:** Stir in the coconut oil and drops of essential oil. The mixture should have a grainy, wet-sand texture.

3. **Mix Together:** Allow your child to mix the ingredients. The consistency might not be perfectly even, which adds to the homemade charm.

4. **Transfer to Container:** Spoon the sugar scrub into a small container. It's okay if the scrub looks unevenly mixed or clumpy.

5. **Decorate (Optional):** The child can decorate the container with stickers or ribbons.

6. **Usage:** The scrub is ready to use during bath time for gentle exfoliation.

This activity is a fun way for children to create a practical and fragrant product, with the child's unique touch making it special.

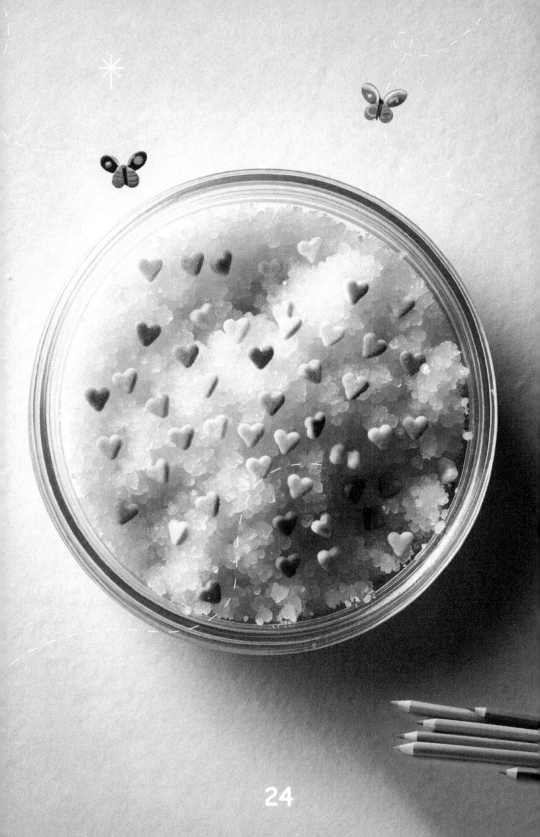

Decorated Photo Frame

Materials

- A simple wooden or cardboard photo frame
- Non-toxic, washable paints in various colors
- Colorful buttons of different sizes
- Newspapers to protect the crafting surface
- Non-toxic glue

Instructions

1. **Paint the Frame:** Let your toddler start by painting the frame with non-toxic, washable paints. They can use different colors and paintbrushes or their fingers to apply the paint. This step doesn't need to be perfect; the charm is in the childlike application of paint.

2. **Add Buttons and Stickers:** Once the paint has dried a bit, it's time to decorate with buttons and stickers. Help your toddler apply glue to the back of the buttons and stick them onto the frame. They can also add stickers wherever they like. Encourage them to be creative with the placement.

3. **Let it Dry:** Set the frame aside to dry completely. Depending on the amount of paint and glue used, this may take several hours.

4. **Final Touches:** Once everything is dry, you can add any additional touches if desired, such as a clear sealant to protect the artwork (this step should be done by an adult).

5. **Add a Photo (Optional):** If you want, insert a special photo into the frame. This could be a picture of the toddler, a family photo, or any other meaningful image.

This craft offers a wonderful way for toddlers to express their creativity and make a meaningful item. It's a great activity for developing fine motor skills and allows for a special bonding experience. Enjoy creating this keepsake together!

Nature Suncatchers

Materials

* Clear contact paper
* Nature items like leaves and flowers
* Paper plate or cardboard ring

Instructions

1. Cut out the center of the paper plate to create a frame.
2. Stick nature items to the contact paper.
3. Place the frame over the decorated contact paper.
4. Hang in a window to catch the light.

Pom-Pom Caterpillar Craft

Materials

✳ A variety of colorful pom-poms in different sizes.

✳ Non-toxic glue.

✳ Small googly eyes.

✳ A piece of sturdy paper or a small wooden stick (for the base).

✳ Optional: Pipe cleaners for antennae.

Instructions

1. **Choose the Pom-Poms:** Let the children select pom-poms to create their caterpillar. They can mix and match colors and sizes to make their caterpillar unique.

2. **Glue the Pom-Poms:** Start gluing the pom-poms in a line on the paper or stick, forming the caterpillar's body. Children should place the larger pom-poms first for the body, gradually using smaller ones towards the end to create a tapered effect.

3. **Add the Eyes:** Once the body is complete, glue the googly eyes onto the first pom-pom to create the caterpillar's face.

4. **Create and Attach Antennae (Optional):** If you're using pipe cleaners for antennae, cut two small pieces and bend them into a suitable shape. Glue these to the top of the first pom-pom.

5. **Let it Dry:** Allow the caterpillar to dry completely. Ensure all the parts are securely attached.

6. **Enjoy Your Caterpillar:** Once dry, the pom-pom caterpillar is ready! It can be a cute decorative piece or a playful toy for the kids.

This craft is not only adorable but also a great way for kids to learn about colors, sequencing, and the natural world in a fun, hands-on way. Enjoy crafting your pom-pom caterpillars!

Beach Gift

Materials

* A beach hat or a small beach bucket
* Non-toxic acrylic paint
* Paint brushes or sponges
* Protective covering for the workspace
* An apron or old clothes for the toddler

Instructions

1. **Prepare the Workspace:** Spread out protective sheets to prevent paint spills. Dress the toddler in an apron or old clothes.

2. **Painting the Hat/Bucket:**
   a. If decorating a beach hat: Place the hat on a flat surface and let the toddler paint it using brushes or sponges. They can make simple strokes or dab colors.
   b. If painting a beach bucket: Hold the bucket securely and let the toddler decorate it with paint.

3. **Embrace Imperfections:** Allow the child to paint freely. Uneven application and paint splashes add to the charm.

4. **Drying:** Let the painted hat or bucket dry completely, which may take a few hours.

5. **Gifting:** Once dry, the hand-decorated beach hat or bucket is ready to be gifted to someone who loves the beach, showcasing the child's creativity and effort.

This craft provides a fun way for a toddler to create a personalized and practical gift for a beach enthusiast.

Painted Sports Water Bottle

Materials

* A clear plastic sports water bottle
* Non-toxic, washable paints or markers suitable for plastic
* Paintbrushes (if using paints)
* Stencils or stickers (optional, for design guidance)
* Newspaper or a plastic sheet (to protect the surface)

Instructions

1. **Prepare Your Workspace:** Cover the area where your toddler will be painting with newspapers or a plastic sheet to protect it.

2. **Decorate the Bottle:** Let your toddler use the paints or markers to decorate the sports water bottle. They can make patterns, draw figures, or simply enjoy splashing colors around. If you're using stickers or stencils, apply them first as guides.

3. **Let it Dry:** Once the decoration is complete, allow the bottle to dry thoroughly. This might take a few hours, depending on the type of paint or marker used.

4. **Remove Stencils or Stickers (If Used):** If you used any stencils or stickers, carefully remove them after the paint is dry.

5. **Ready to Gift:** After everything is completely dry, the personalized sports water bottle is ready to be gifted. It's a practical and thoughtful gift for anyone who loves to stay hydrated during their workouts.

This craft is not only an enjoyable activity for a toddler but also creates a unique and useful gift for someone passionate about fitness. Enjoy the crafting process!

Rocky Bug Garden

Materials

* Small stones or pebbles
* Non-toxic paint in various colors
* Googly eyes (optional, can also use painted eyes)
* Cardboard or a small wooden plank for the base
* Markers or paint pens
* Glue

Instructions

1. **Stone Selection:** Have the toddler pick out a variety of stones, preferably in different shapes and sizes that could resemble bugs' bodies.

2. **Painting Stones:** Let the toddler paint the stones in various colors. It doesn't have to be neat; messy and overlapping colors add character to the bugs.

3. **Adding Details:** Once the stones are dry, toddlers can use markers or paint pens to add stripes, dots, or any designs they like. They can be haphazard and irregular for a more 'ugly bug' effect.

4. **Creating Faces:** If using googly eyes, help the toddler glue them onto the stones to create faces. If not, they can paint on eyes, mouths, etc.

5. **Assembling the Garden:** Glue the painted bugs onto the cardboard or wooden plank. The arrangement can be random, like bugs scattered in a garden.

6. **Display:** The rocky bug garden can be placed outdoors in the family garden or indoors as a fun conversation piece.

This craft allows for a lot of creative freedom and is meant to be more about the process than the final look. It's a great way to engage a child's imagination and motor skills.

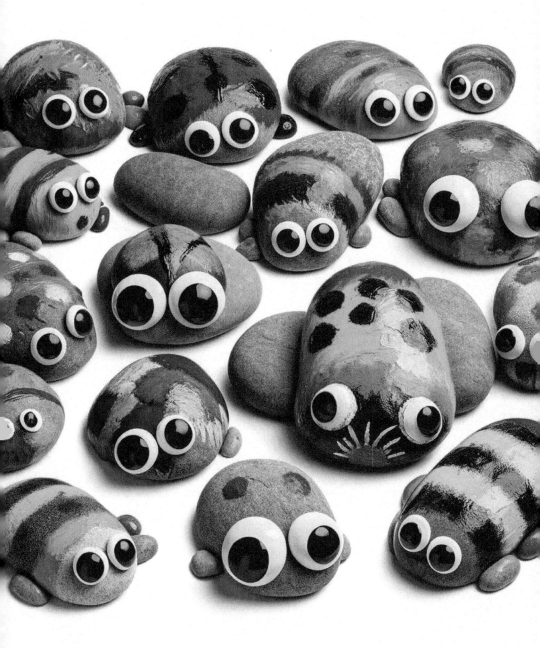

Yarn-Wrapped Sticks

Materials

* Sticks of various lengths
* Yarn in different colors
* Scissors

Instructions

1. **Gather Sticks:** Collect some sticks from outside; they can be of varying lengths and thicknesses.

2. **Cut Yarn:** Cut lengths of yarn in various colors.

3. **Start Wrapping:** Choose a stick and a color to start with. Tie one end of the yarn to the stick.

4. **Wrap the Yarn:** Wrap the yarn around the stick. Overlap and switch colors randomly.

5. **Secure the Yarn:** When you're done with a color, tie the end to another piece of yarn or tuck it under the wrapped layers.

6. **Display:** Once all sticks are wrapped, display them in a vase or tie them together to hang on the wall.

Let the child wrap the sticks freely for an authentic, 'made by a child' look.

Painted Apron

Materials

* A plain apron
* Non-toxic fabric paint in a limited color palette
* Paintbrushes or sponges
* Protective covering for the workspace
* An apron or old clothes for the child

Instructions

1. **Prepare the Workspace:** Cover the area with protective sheets to avoid paint spills. Dress the child in an apron or old clothes.

2. **Painting the Apron:** Let the child use paintbrushes or sponges to apply paint to the apron. They can make handprints, dab colors, or paint simple shapes.

3. **Embrace Imperfections:** Encourage the child to have fun. Paint splashes and uneven application add to the charm.

4. **Drying:** Allow the apron to dry completely. Follow the fabric paint instructions for drying and setting the paint.

5. **Gifting:** Once dry, the apron is ready to be gifted, showcasing the child's creativity and effort.

This craft provides a delightful way for a toddler to create a personalized and practical gift.

Baseball Gift

Materials

* A baseball or a small wooden baseball bat
* Non-toxic acrylic paint
* Paint brushes or sponges
* Protective covering for the workspace
* An apron or old clothes for the toddler

Instructions

1. **Prepare the Workspace:** Lay down protective sheets to prevent paint spills. Dress the toddler in an apron or old clothes to protect them from paint stains.

2. **Painting the Baseball/Bat:**
   a. If painting a baseball: Let the toddler hold the ball as they paint it. Encourage them to use colors and make simple designs or strokes.
   b. If decorating a baseball bat: Hold the bat securely and let the toddler decorate the handle or a small section with paint.

3. **Embrace Imperfections:** Allow the child to paint freely. Imperfect and uneven paint application adds character and charm.

4. **Drying:** Let the painted baseball or bat dry completely. This may take a few hours.

5. **Gifting:** Once dry, the baseball or bat is ready to be gifted to someone who loves baseball, showcasing the child's creativity and effort.

This craft provides a fun way for a toddler to create a personalized gift for a baseball enthusiast, capturing their unique touch and creativity.

Minimalist Leaf Prints

Materials

* White canvas
* Black non-toxic paint
* A variety of leaves with interesting shapes

Instructions

1. Paint one side of each leaf with black paint.
2. Press the painted side onto the canvas to create a print.
3. Repeat with different leaves to create a pattern.
4. Allow the prints to dry for a natural yet sophisticated art piece.

Chic Monochrome Handprints

Materials

* White cardstock
* Non-toxic black paint
* Picture frame

Instructions

1. Help your toddler cover their hand with black paint. Press their hand onto the white cardstock to create a handprint.

2. Repeat to make a pattern, or keep it to one for simplicity.

3. Frame the dried handprint art for a chic black-and-white piece.

Decorated Coffee Mug

Materials

* A plain white ceramic mug
* Non-toxic, washable ceramic paints or markers (safe for children)
* Paintbrushes (if using paints)
* Stencils or stickers (optional, for design guidance)

Instructions

1. **Prepare the Mug:** Make sure the mug is clean and dry before starting. If you're using stencils or stickers for design guidance, place them on the mug first.

2. **Decorate the Mug:** Let your toddler decorate the mug using the ceramic paints or markers. They can draw, dab, or create patterns. Encourage them to express their creativity, keeping in mind that the designs will be unique and not perfect.

3. **Let it Dry:** Once your toddler is done decorating, let the mug dry completely. The drying time will depend on the type of paints or markers used, so refer to the product instructions.

4. **Seal the Design (Optional):** For longevity, you might want to seal the design. Some ceramic paints or markers require baking the mug in the oven to set the design. Follow the product instructions carefully for this step.

5. **Ready to Gift:** After the mug is completely dry (and baked if necessary), it's ready to be gifted. This personalized mug, decorated by a toddler, will surely bring a smile to any coffee lover's face.

This craft not only offers a fun and engaging activity for toddlers but also results in a thoughtful and unique gift. Enjoy crafting with your little one!

49

Handmade Bookmark

Materials

* Colorful paper (construction paper is ideal)
* Non-toxic glue
* Large glitter or sequins
* Playful stickers
* Non-toxic paint (for the handprint)

Instructions

1. **Cut the Paper:** Start by cutting a strip of colorful paper to make the bookmark. It doesn't need to be perfectly straight or evenly cut — the charm is in its imperfection. A good size is about 2 inches wide and 6 inches long, but you can adjust this based on preference.

2. **Handprint Decoration:** Pour a small amount of non-toxic paint onto a plate. Help your toddler press their hand into the paint and then carefully onto the paper to leave a handprint. Allow it to dry completely.

3. **Add Glitter and Stickers:** Once the handprint is dry, apply small dots of glue over the bookmark and let your toddler sprinkle large glitter or place sequins on these spots. They can also add stickers to decorate the bookmark further. This part is all about letting them be creative!

4. **Dry and Use:** Let the bookmark dry thoroughly. Once it's dry, it's ready to be used or gifted to a reading enthusiast!

This activity is not only a fun craft for a toddler but also results in a charming and personal gift for any book lover. Remember, the beauty of this craft lies in its simplicity and the joy it brings to both the creator and the receiver. Enjoy your crafting time!

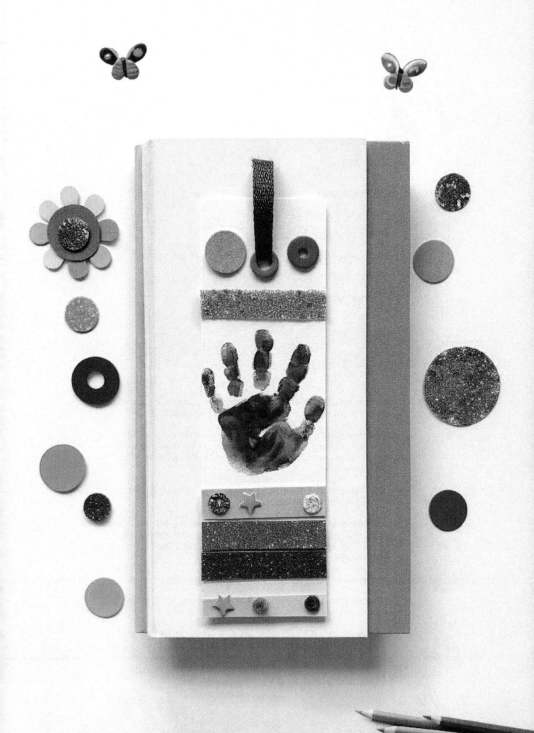

Paw Print Art

Materials

* Non-toxic, washable paint (safe for pets)
* Plain white paper or canvas
* A pet's paw (dog or cat)
* Wipes or a damp cloth (for cleaning the pet's paw)
* A small, shallow dish or plate
* A frame (optional)

Instructions

1. **Prep the Paint:** Pour some non-toxic paint into the shallow dish. Spread it out so the pet's paw can easily be dipped into it.

2. **Paw Print:** Gently press your pet's paw into the paint, ensuring it's evenly coated. Then, carefully press the painted paw onto the paper or canvas. You might need to do this a few times to get a clear print.

3. **Clean Up:** Immediately clean your pet's paw with wipes or a damp cloth to remove all paint.

4. **Decorating:** Let your toddler add decorations around the paw print, like hearts or stars, using the same or different paint colors. Remember, it doesn't need to be perfect. The charm is in the toddler's touch.

5. **Drying:** Allow the art to dry completely.

6. **Framing:** Once dry, you can frame the artwork, making it a perfect gift for any pet lover.

7. **Gifting:** Present the paw print art as a gift, highlighting the special bond between the pet and its owner.

This craft not only provides a fun activity for the toddler but also creates a unique keepsake for someone who cherishes their pet.

Popsicle Stick Star Ornament

Materials

* 5-20 popsicle sticks per star.
* Non-toxic glue.
* Non-toxic paint and paintbrush (optional).
* Ribbon or string for hanging.
* Newspapers or a plastic sheet (for protecting the surface).

Instructions

1. **Arrange the Popsicle Sticks:** Lay out the popsicle sticks in a star shape on your workspace. Each end of a stick should overlap with the next to form the points of the star.

2. **Glue the Sticks Together:** Apply glue at each point of overlap. Press the sticks together gently and let the glue set for a few minutes. For younger toddlers, an adult may need to help with this step.

3. **Paint the Star (Optional):** Once the glue is dry, you can paint the star in a color of your choice. This step is optional but adds a modern touch to the ornament.

4. **Add the Hanging Mechanism:** Tie a ribbon or string around one of the points of the star for hanging. You can also glue the ribbon to the back of the star.

5. **Let it Dry Completely:** If you painted the star, allow ample time for the paint to dry before hanging.

6. **Display the Ornament:** Your popsicle stick star ornament is now ready to be displayed! It can be hung on a wall, a window, or even a Christmas tree.

This craft is great for toddlers as it's simple yet allows for creative expression. The star ornament can be a lovely addition to home decor or a handmade gift. Enjoy crafting together!

Toddler-Friendly Popsicle Stick Picture Frame

Materials

* Popsicle sticks (around 4-8 depending on the desired size)
* Non-toxic glue
* Non-toxic paint and paintbrushes (optional)
* Stickers or other simple decorations (optional)
* A photo or drawing to place inside the frame

Instructions

1. **Layout the Popsicle Sticks:** Lay out four popsicle sticks to form a square or rectangular shape. This will be the base of your frame.

2. **Glue the Sticks Together:** Apply glue to the ends of each stick where they overlap. Press them together gently to form the frame. For a more secure frame, glue additional sticks across the back of the frame in a horizontal or vertical direction.

3. **Paint and Decorate (Optional):** Once the glue is dry, you can paint the frame in different colors. Let your toddler choose their favorite colors and paint the sticks. After the paint dries, they can further decorate the frame with stickers or by drawing on it with markers.

4. **Insert the Picture:** Once all decorations are dry, tape a photo or drawing to the back of the frame.

5. **Display the Frame:** Now your popsicle stick picture frame is ready to be displayed or gifted! It can stand on its own or be attached to a wall or fridge.

This craft is great for toddlers as it allows them to be creative and make something functional. It's also a wonderful way to display their artwork or a special photo. Enjoy crafting together!

Sparkling Diamond Art

Materials

* Sheets of paper (white or colored)
* Assorted faux diamonds or rhinestones (various sizes and colors)
* Non-toxic glue
* A tray or container to hold the diamonds

Instructions

1. **Prepare the Workspace:** Set up a crafting area and place the diamonds in a tray or container for easy access.

2. **Apply Glue:** Help your toddler apply glue to the paper in the areas where they want to place the diamonds. They can make dots, lines, or shapes with the glue.

3. **Stick the Diamonds:** Let your toddler pick up the diamonds and stick them onto the glued areas on the paper. They can create any design they like - random patterns, shapes, or even a simple picture.

4. **Let it Dry:** Once they're done decorating, set the artwork aside to dry. Make sure all the diamonds are firmly in place.

5. **Display the Artwork:** After the glue has dried, the sparkling diamond art is ready to be displayed. It can be a beautiful addition to your home decor or a special gift.

This craft allows toddlers to explore their creativity and practice fine motor skills, all while having fun with the sparkle and shine of the diamonds. Enjoy this glittering crafting activity!

Lavender Bath Salt

Materials

* Epsom salts
* Lavender essential oil
* Small jars
* Ribbon
* Bowl and spoon for mixing

Instructions

1. **Mix the Salts:** In a bowl, help your child mix a desired amount of Epsom salts with a few drops of lavender essential oil. Stir well until the oil is evenly distributed.

2. **Add Color (Optional):** If you want to add color, a few drops of food coloring can be mixed in.

3. **Fill the Jars:** Allow your child to spoon the salt mixture into the small jars. They might fill them unevenly, which adds to the charm.

4. **Decorate with Ribbon:** Cut lengths of ribbon and tie them around the necks of the jars. The bows or knots can be simple and a bit messy.

5. **Gift or Use:** These homemade lavender bath salts can be used for a relaxing bath or given as a unique, child-made gift.

This craft allows children to engage in a simple, sensory activity, creating something both useful and fragrant, with the added charm of their unique touch.

Glitter Glue Art

Materials

* Sheets of paper (white or colored)
* Various colors of glitter glue
* A workspace cover (newspapers or a plastic sheet)

Instructions

1. **Prepare the Workspace:** Cover your crafting area with newspapers or a plastic sheet to protect surfaces from glitter glue spills.

2. **Select Glitter Glue:** Let your toddler choose their favorite colors of glitter glue.

3. **Create the Artwork:** Encourage your toddler to squeeze the glitter glue onto the paper to create designs. They can make lines, dots, swirls, or any abstract shapes. There's no right or wrong way to do this; it's all about creative expression.

4. **Let it Dry:** Once they are done with their design, set the paper aside to dry. Glitter glue can take a while to dry completely, so patience is key.

5. **Display the Artwork:** After the glitter glue has dried, you can display your toddler's artwork. It can be hung on the wall, placed on a shelf, or even given as a gift to family and friends.

This craft is a fantastic way for toddlers to explore colors and textures while practicing their fine motor skills. The glittery outcome is sure to delight them! Enjoy this sparkling crafting activity.

Wooden Bead Bracelet

Materials

* Wooden beads (various sizes and colors)
* String or yarn
* Scissors

Instructions

1. **Prepare Beads:** If painting beads, let them dry after painting.

2. **Cut String:** For a necklace, about 24–30 inches; for a bracelet, 8–10 inches.

3. **String Beads:** Tie a knot at one end of the string, then thread the beads.

4. **Finish:** Tie the ends together once all beads are on.

5. **Trim Excess:** Leave a small tail to prevent unraveling.

This craft is a fun and creative way for kids to make beautiful jewelry, perfect as a gift or personal accessory.

Herb Salt Mix

Materials

* Coarse salt (like sea salt or kosher salt)
* Dried herbs (such as rosemary, thyme, basil, or lavender)
* A clean, dry glass bottle or jar with a lid
* A bowl for mixing
* A spoon or small scoop
* Optional: ribbon or label for decoration

Instructions

1. **Choose Herbs and Salt:** Let your child select their choice of dried herbs. You can use a single herb or a combination.

2. **Mix the Herbs and Salt:** In a bowl, help your child mix the coarse salt with the dried herbs. A good ratio is about 3 parts salt to 1 part herbs, but you can adjust this according to taste.

3. **Fill the Bottle:** Once the herbs and salt are well mixed, use the spoon or scoop to carefully fill the glass bottle with the mixture.

4. **Decorate the Bottle:** Decorate the bottle with a ribbon or attach a label. Your child can write the name of the mix or a message on the label.

It's a great way to introduce children to natural seasonings and the joy of creating something that can be used in everyday cooking.

Clay Candle Holder

Materials

- Air-dry clay
- Rolling pin
- Circular object (for base shape, like a jar or can)
- Small cookie cutters or a straw (to create holes)
- Sandpaper (fine-grit, optional for smoothing)
- Optional: Craft knife (for shaping) Paint and brushes (for decoration), Sealant (for protection)

Instructions

1. **Roll the Clay:** Knead and roll out the clay to 1/4 inch thickness.

2. **Cut the Base:** Use a circular object to cut out the base.

3. **Form the Cylinder:** Cut a rectangle for the cylinder wall. Make holes using a straw or cutters.

4. **Assemble:** Attach the wall to the base, forming a cylinder. Smooth edges and let dry as per clay instructions.

5. **Sand and Decorate** (Optional): Sand rough edges. Paint and apply sealant if desired.

This craft allows children to explore shapes and patterns while creating a functional and beautiful item. The candle holder, with its glowing patterns of light, makes a charming addition to any room or a thoughtful gift.

Clay Jewelry Holder

Materials

* Air-dry clay
* Rolling pin
* Knife or clay cutting tool
* Optional: Paint and brushes (for decoration), Sealant (for protection)

Instructions

1. **Prepare the Clay:** Knead the air-dry clay until it's soft. Use a rolling pin to flatten it out to about 1/2 inch thickness for the base.

2. **Create the Base:** Cut a shape for the base, like a circle or square, from the flattened clay.

3. **Form Holders:** Roll additional clay into tubes or shape into cones for ring holders. For necklace holders, make taller posts. These should be thick enough to support jewelry without tipping over.

4. **Attach Holders to Base:** Press the bottom of each tube or cone firmly onto the base. Smooth the edges where they join for stability.

5. **Let it Dry:** Allow the clay to dry thoroughly, according to the manufacturer's instructions, usually 24-48 hours.

6. **Paint (Optional):** Once dry, your child can paint the jewelry holder. Let the paint dry completely. **Apply Sealant (Optional):** To protect the paint and clay, apply a sealant and let it dry.

Pencil Holder

Materials

* Air-dry clay
* Small bowl or cup (for molding)
* Plastic knife (for details)
* Paint and brushes
* Sealant (optional)

Instructions

1. **Mold Clay:** Knead air-dry clay and wrap around a small bowl to form a cylinder.

2.

3. **Add Flower:** Shape a simple flower onto the front using a plastic knife.

4. **Dry:** Remove from the mold and let dry as instructed by the clay's packaging.

5. **Paint:** Decorate the holder and flower with paint; let dry.

6. **Seal (Optional):** Apply sealant for durability.

Your child's charming pencil holder is all set, making a delightful and personal gift for someone special.

Printed in Great Britain
by Amazon